SAN FRANCISCO

Text by
ROSANNA CIRIGLIANO - RICHARD FREMANTLE

Photos by
ANDREA PISTOLESI

BB
BONECHI
SNC

INDEX

Publication created and designed by Casa Editrice Bonechi
Project and graphic realization: Monica Bonechi
New edition revision and layout: ARA Fototecnica
Editing: Simonetta Giorgi

Text: Rosanna Cirigliano - Richard Fremantle

Map: Daniela Mariani

© Copyright by Casa Editrice Bonechi, Via Cairoli 18/b - I - 50131 Florence

ISBN 978-88-8029-478-8

Golden Gate Bridge.

THE MISTRESS OF THEM ALL

San Francisco is one of the most beautiful cities in the world. Of the great bay cities — Hong Kong, Sidney, Manila, Singapore, New York, Rio, Naples — it's maybe the most beautiful of all.

A mild climate, cosmopolitan people from all over the world and an incredibly gorgeous setting distance it from even its closest rivals. It's America's Pacific capital.

Art, wonderful architecture, music of every sort — opera, pop, symphonic, rock — fantastic food, some of the best local wines in the world, old-style banking and modern electronics, big film-makers and small post-production studios, record companies, chic clothing manufacturers, the American West and the Pacific East — San Francisco is a crossroads of many things and many diverse people happily living side by side, feeling no compulsion to change the others or to be changed by them.

San Francisco is on the northern end of a peninsula which has, to the west, the Pacific Ocean, to the north, the straits into San Francisco Bay called the Golden Gate and, to the east, San Francisco Bay. The city is about seven miles long and seven miles wide, some 49 square miles, which may be compared to the roughly 46 square miles of Manhattan.

It's the central hub of a vast area which includes, northwards, the Pacific coast, Seattle, Vancouver, and Alaska. To the east are Salt Lake City, Denver, Omaha, and Kansas City. To the south, Los Angeles, San Diego, Baja California and Mexico. To the west many spokes reach out into the Pacific: to Sidney and Auckland, Singapore, Manila, Hanoi, Hong Kong, Taiwan, Tokyo, as well as to the islands of Hawaii.

In San Francisco all these spokes and all these influences come together.

And, of course, San Francisco is the hub of a much smaller wheel, made up of California and the Bay Area. Not that California, the richest American state, with some twenty-five million people, roughly twice the land area of Great Britain, stunning scenery everywhere, and an economy among the world's top ten, is exactly a small hub. . .

San Francisco itself has a population of some 800,000 people. But the Bay Area is enormous —

3

over 50 miles long and almost 20 wide, with a total population of over 5,000,000 around the two sections of the Bay — San Francisco Bay to the south and east of San Francisco itself, and San Pablo Bay to the north.

South, past San Francisco airport, are *Burlingame, San Mateo, Palo Alto* — with the world-renowned *Stanford University* — *Los Altos, Los Gatos, Santa Clara,* and *San Jose*. A lot of the most southern part of the Bay is now involved in the electronics industries — computers, lasers, optics and the like. South of San Jose, in *Santa Clara, San Benito* and *Monterey Counties*, there are many ranches, orchards and wineries.

Across the Bay from San Francisco are *Newark, Fremont, Union City, Hayward, Castro Valley, San Leandro, Walnut Creek,* and, of course, *Oakland*. To the northeast are *Berkeley,* with the other great university of the Bay Area, *Richmond, San Pablo, Pinole, Martinez* and *Vallejo*. North from Vallejo begins the famous *Napa* and *Sonoma* wine country. Directly north, across the Golden Gate Bridge, are the elegant suburban towns in beautiful Marin County — *Belvedere, Sausalito, Tiburon, Larkspur, Mill Valley,* and *San Rafael. Muir Woods National Monument* with its 1,000-year old redwoods, the *Point Reyes National Seashore,* and the new *Golden Gate Seashore Community Center,* on the land at the *Headlands* saved from speculative residential development through the efforts of a few public-spirited San Franciscans, are also across Golden Gate Bridge.

San Francisco's unique character and great beauty come from its position on the slim peninsula nearly surrounded by water — 5,000 miles of Pacific to Tokyo on one side and 3,000 miles of the American continent on the other, to New York. The city overlooks the ocean, guards the Golden Gate, and dominates the Bay.

In San Francisco you smell the salt air and feel the energy of the sea. The light invigorates and dazzles against the city's forty-odd hills covered in green parks, wide streets and bright buildings, changing as the sun moves over them. It's a clean, brisk, young city, full of open, almost blatant enthusiasm. When you look out across the beautiful, blue expanse of the Bay, the wind-filled white and multi-colored sails seem like a wonderful piece of fantasy — kinetic and poor-art and earth-art all mixed in a perpetual free-show, private for San Franciscans only. And then, just to keep the show unpredictable, San Francisco's famous Bay mist will move in off the ocean,

A bird's-eye view of the city, the Golden Gate Bridge and the San Francisco-Oakland Bay Bridge.

swirling around the towers of the Golden Gate Bridge to envelop the water and the city, blocking out the sun and chilling everyone and everything. The city's character is also made by its layered quality. Most cities are stitched against a common cloth — London is English, Paris French, Rome Italian, Beijing Chinese — but San Francisco has no such steady base. It's a city unlike any other, a tolerant city which prides itself on appreciating novelty, a *different* city as any San Franciscan will tell you. Its history is like thin layers, each lying on top of the last with very little mixture. Today San Francisco bears no resemblance to the World War II U.S. Navy port of the 40s, or the earthquake city of 1906, or the San Francisco of the Gold Rush.

The lowest layer, the one before any men lived on San Francisco Bay, before in fact even the Bay or the lovely hills around it existed, is the most exciting layer, the frightening one, a risk-layer every day for every San Franciscan. It's the earthquake layer.

The San Francisco Bay Area sits squarely on the so-called San Andreas Fault, part of the great Pacific Basin where 80% of the world's earthquakes start. On April 18, 1906, early in the morning, San Francisco experienced a massive earthquake that killed over 500 people and destroyed, together with the fire that followed it, much of the city. Since these major earthquakes seem to happen in the San Francisco area every 100 years or so, and since, as someone once put it, 'The further you are from the last one, the nearer you are to the next', each day the risk for San Franciscans goes up just a little. It's a bit like living on a cliff and watching it slowly crumble away under your feet. Scary, but part of what makes the city so exciting even for visitors.

The next layer is the water layer because San Francisco is a city of water and what water provides — oysters and shrimp, crab, wonderful fish and even, in the mixed fresh and saltwater of the San Joaquin and Sacramento Rivers, sturgeon with their famous caviar. There's boating, surfing and swimming galore, sunbathing on the Pacific beaches and of course, everywhere, the good energy that living by water always imparts.

The land layer above the ocean layer and the bays, includes the hills in the city, and all around on the landward sides, with wonderful vistas — the *Sonoma*, the *Diablo* and the *Santa Cruz* ranges. Even the town's hills go up to over 900 feet.

The picturesque Victorian houses, Fisherman's Wharf and a view of the Golden Gate.

The Golden Gate is one of the longest bridges in the world.

HISTORY OF SAN FRANCISCO

Early European and American settlers coming across the Continent from the east must have thought they'd arrived in the Garden of Eden, so enchanting is the edge of the Pacific around San Francisco.

Indians were the first people we know who lived in the Bay Area — Pomos, Wintums, Yokuts, Costanoans, Wapas, and Miwoks. They were mostly undisturbed by Europeans until 1776. That year the Spanish who claimed all of Alta California, together with most of the southwest United States, no doubt fearing the inevitable expansion of the Anglo-Americans, established a settlement where San Francisco now is and called it *Yerba Buena*, after the mint which grew wild in the area. The colony had a Catholic Mission church called *Dolores*, and there was a *presidio*, a small fort to defend the entrance to the Bay. But already in 1776, Spain's American empire was in deep trouble everywhere so the new colony neither prospered nor existed for very long. In 1821 Mexico declared its independence from Spain. California became Mexican. Then in 1846 an American Navy sloop called *Portsmouth* seized the run-down fort and little settlement at *Yerba Buena*. A war ensued. Under the Americans *Yerba Buena* became *San Francisco*. Only two years later, in 1848, just as the war between Mexico and the U.S. was ending and California was becoming American, a fellow named James Marshall found gold at Sutter's Mill. The *Gold Rush*, the next significant moment in San Francisco's layers of history, was on.

For a few years the town grew by leaps and
bounds. Between 1847 and 1850, San Francisco
grew from a few hundred people to an estimated
25,000. It became known as one of the wickedest
towns on earth, the *Barbary Coast* — fast living
and fast dying. But then the gold gave out, and
the city's development became more steady.
Slowly it developed great wealth, based on the
trade of the port, on silver which was found in
Nevada in enormous quantities, and on the arrival
of the railroads.
This century the main layers in San Francisco's
history have been: the 'quake' of 1906; the
opening of the San Francisco-Oakland Bay Bridge
and the Golden Gate Bridge in 1936 and 1937; the
Second World War when the city became a pivot
for American efforts in the Pacific; the '50s and
'60s when San Francisco became one of the
centers of *beat* and then *hip* and *hippy* culture;

and the '70s and '80s when it became the financial
center for the electronics industries in particular,
and the enormous growth of California in general.
Finally, in the 1980s, San Francisco, which had
always thought of itself as a city on the edge of
the American Continent, began thinking of itself as
a city on the rim of the Pacific Ocean — the
center, in fact, of American interests in the whole
Pacific area.
San Francisco's population today reflects an ethnic
separateness and toleration which is unique, like a
vertical version of the historical layering.
American Indians, black Americans and white,
Chinese, Filippinos, Hawaiians, Japanese, people
from all over the Pacific, from the Caribbean,
from Europe, from Mexico — all live next to each
other, retaining their ethnic identity, but each also
being a San Franciscan.
The Gay community of San Francisco, for

Above, *a bird's-eye view of the city,* right *an evening shot of the Golden Gate Bridge.*

example, is probably the world's largest and most sophisticated — precisely because of this mutual toleration among differing life-styles.

San Francisco is a great center for finance, as much for the western U.S. as for the Pacific. It's an artistic and cultural city without many peers in North America, where every kind of music flourishes, where old museums and new art galleries reflect the growing importance of the visual arts. The city's becoming increasingly important in the film industry. Its restaurants rival any in the world, while many of its wines from the nearby Napa and Sonoma regions are unequalled anywhere. Shops in San Francisco are among the best in the western United States and, because the city is one of those rare and wonderful ones in the States, where it is a pleasure to walk, shopping is a delightful pastime.

Besides all that, San Francisco's wonderful, sunny, open-air existence, its many parks, particularly the *Golden Gate Park*, which is the largest man-made park in the world, together with the beautiful country across the Golden Gate and San Francisco-Oakland Bay Bridges, the water everywhere for swimming and sailing, the beaches, the islands, all continue to give San Francisco a lovely and healthy, open-air lifestyle, unique among the great cities of the world.

San Francisco also has *Fisherman's Wharf* and the *Marina,* its fishing fleet, *Chinatown,* the *Haight-Ashbury* district, the *Presidio,* cable cars, old houses and new skyscrapers, magnificent views and a myriad of other wonderful things. But above all else, the city is made by its friendly, energetic and intelligent people.

San Francisco is maybe the most delightful, liveable, visitable city in the world.

So enjoy it!

Mission Dolores.

MISSION DOLORES

The small structure to the left of the above photograph represents an integral part of San Francisco's history. Mission San Francisco de Asis, or **Mission Dolores** as it has always been called, was founded in 1776 as one of 21 missions established by Spanish Franciscan fathers in California, from San Diego in the south to Sonoma in the north. Father Juniper Serra directed this drive to convert the local Indians, fully supported by Spanish colonial authorities seeking to reinforce their temporal power. Lieutenant Colonel Juan Bautista de Anza selected the site for the San Francisco (then known as Yerba Buena) mission next to a stream which he called Arroyo de los Dolores, Our Lady of Sorrows, whose feast day it happened to be.

The name was used for a nearby lake (since filled-in), and later the mission.

Mission Dolores has been extensively restored so that its original appearance remains intact, including four-foot adobe walls, a timbered ceiling painted with vegetable dyes and held together with rawhide, and altar decorations brought from Spain and Mexico. The large church to the right of the simple edifice, the Mission Dolores Basilica, is of more recent origin. It was rebuilt in 1919 in a wedding cake Spanish/Moorish style, and raised to the status of a basilica in 1952 by Pope Pius XII.

A statue of Father Serra also graces the grounds, and a cemetery containing the remains of early settlers is nearby.

City Hall.

CIVIC CENTER

The institutional heart of San Francisco, the **Civic Center**, is a group of expressly-designed federal, state and city buildings.

Early in the 20th century, city planner Daniel Burnham envisaged a bold, large-scale architectural complex for San Francisco. The earthquake of 1906, which buried the old City Hall, conveniently cleared the field for his dream, realized only after his death. His ideals were carried forward by Arthur Brown Jr., the architect for the new **City Hall**. Brown attended the École des Beaux Arts in Paris, and returned to the U.S. to design a spectacular Beaux Arts style

City Hall with the support of San Francisco Mayor Sunny Jim Rolph. The building is a model of grandeur, and is topped by a dome taller than that of the U.S. Capitol. San Franciscans come here to pay their taxes, while visitors take private and guided tours to admire the stately surroundings which have borne silent witness to demonstrations, state funerals, banquets and celebrations.

The Beaux Arts design extends to the other structures in the complex, including the **War Memorial Opera House**, where representatives from 50 nations signed the United Nations

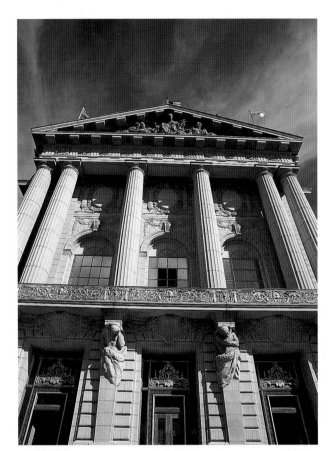

founding charter in 1945. The War Memorial Opera House, Davies Hall, the War Memorial Veterans Building and the Ballet Building of the Civic Center are united under the single title of the **San Francisco War Memorial and Performing Arts Center**. The most recent addition (1980) to the Civic Center, the **Louise M. Davies Symphony Hall** breaks the general Beaux Arts theme with a modern design expressed in glass. The San Francisco Symphony holds concerts in this building from October to May.

The Civic Center also contains the Public Library, the Federal Building, the Federal Office Building, the State Office Building, and the Public Utilities Commision headquarters, all in the more classical style. On a lighter note, the **Civic Center Plaza** hosts an open-air exhibition of paintings, sculptures and crafts every September.

Detail of the City Hall decorated in the Beaux Arts style of architecture.

Below, *view from on high of the Civic Center.*

The facade of the War Memorial Opera House; the statue dedicated to the early explorers and pioneers of California, donated to the city in 1894 by James Lick; the statue of Abraham Lincoln and the Louise Davies Symphony Hall.

LINCOLN
ERECTED BY PVBLIC SVBSCRIPTION
VNDER THE AVSPICES OF THE LINCOLN
MONVMENT LEAGVE REPRESENTING
THE GRAND ARMY OF THE REPVBLIC
& THE LINCOLN GRAMMAR SCHOOL
ASSOCIATION OF SAN FRANCISCO

MCMXXVII

Above, *the financial district*, right, *the Transamerica Pyramid.*

FINANCIAL DISTRICT

Much of the Pacific coast along with a steady proportion of world commerce hums to the rhythm of San Francisco's Financial District, which had its origins in the Gold Rush of 1849 and was built on. . . landfill!

The Gold Rush started in a modest way: a New Jersey carpenter, James Marshall, found a nugget of gold while constructing a sawmill on property belonging to John Sutter, outside San Francisco. The word spread like wildfire, and the population of the town exploded overnight. The boom was on.

Gold diggers arrived by boat at Yerba Buena Cove. They covered the cove's mud flats with sand, and a sea wall was constructed so ships could load and unload their cargo directly onto wharves. Eventually, the ex-mud flats and the area up to the sea wall were filled with land from some of the city's smaller hills. This is where the first banking offices were set up to handle the assets of the Gold Rush, and silver from Nevada's Comstock Lode, in the 1850s and '60s.

Perhaps San Francisco's most famous banker was A.P. Giannini who opened the Bank of Italy at the turn of the century. During the earthquake of 1906, Giannini hid the bank's deposits in a fruit and vegetable wagon, and was one of the first banking officials to honor withdrawals from customers after the disaster. The Bank of Italy eventually turned into the **Bank of America;** its corporate headquarters in San Francisco are located in a 52 story red carnelian marble skyscraper. The building which stands out among the tall silhouettes housing insurance, corporate and international banking offices is the 48 story **Transamerica Pyramid**. Designed by a Los Angeles firm, the pyramid has turned into a symbol of San Francisco, to the chagrin of the natives. One saving grace is a small space planted with redwoods at its eastern base.

The high-rise cityscape of San Francisco is mainly the result of a zoning code passed in 1968, which allowed tall, flat-topped buildings for the first time. The profusion of modernistic skyscrapers that followed in the Financial District is presently being regulated by a Downtown Plan meant to establish esthetic controls and guidelines. One low-lying edifice in the heart of the Financial District remains the **Stock Exchange**, constructed in 1930 in a classical architectural style.

The modern Transamerica Pyramid contrasted with an older victorian style building.

Right, the futuristic architecture of the Embarcadero and the Vaillancourt Fountain.

THE EMBARCADERO CENTER

East of the Financial District is a spectacular complex known as the **Embarcadero Center**. Its pillars are four skyscrapers, plus a signature Hyatt Regency hotel; pedestrian walkways above street level connect each building. Down and around, there is a multi-level arcade filled with shops and restaurants. Another outstanding feature of the Embarcadero Center is a variety of outdoor sculptures. Probably, the **Vaillancourt Fountain**, a sort of urban Stonehenge is the most well-known of the group. Visitors can follow a series of stepping-stones across a reflecting pool and walk through piles of concrete boxes that make up the sculpture while listening to water sounds without getting wet. Other notable sculptures range from Bufano animals to abstract works by Willi Gutmann and Louise Nevelson.

Union Square: the statue of Victory.

UNION SQUARE

This downtown area is the city Mecca for
shoppers. It is filled with antique and jewelry
shops, art galleries, small boutiques and large
department stores including I. Magnin, Neiman
Marcus, and Macy's. The heart of the district is
Union Square, a 2.6 acre park resplendent with
palm and yew trees, box hedges, flowers, and
stone benches. The surroundings do not speak of
war; yet a statue of Victory atop a granite column
commemorates Admiral Dewey's triumph at
Manila Bay during the Spanish-American War.
And the square itself, presented to the city in 1850
by Mayor Geary, received its name from a
number of pro-Union rallies held there
during the Civil War.

Today, Union Square is home to flower vendors (who have been part of the local scene since the early 1900s), street artists, musicians, and flocks of pigeons. The square is set over an enormous underground parking garage, handy for shoppers, many of whom head for nearby **Maiden Lane**, a street lined with exclusive boutiques. One would never guess that it was called Morton Street up to the earthquake, famed for its bawdy houses. Destruction, new name, new life.

Another favorite with shoppers is the **Crocker Galleria**, a glass barrel-vaulted arcade reminiscent of Milan's Galleria Vittorio Emanuele. Boutiques and specialty shops are once again the order of the day, with the spotlight on contemporary design.

At the side, *the entrance to the Neiman-Marcus department store;* below, *the glass vault of the Crocker Galleria.*

CHINATOWN

Not far away from the Crocker Galleria is the **Ceremonial Gateway** to San Francisco's **Chinatown**, topped by two grimacing dragons, at Grant and Bush Streets. The gate is more than merely symbolic, for one enters another world, that of the largest Chinese enclave outside Asia. Chinese-American residents here number nearly 80,000, roughly one-tenth of San Francisco's population. The immediate impression is one of color and compactness: the reds, greens, oranges and yellows of banners, signs and pagoda roofs overlook shop premises jammed with ivory, jade, cloisonné, porcelain, teak and bamboo trinkets and treasures, or fresh produce, meats, herbs, and teas. Needless to say, dining in Chinatown is an experience not to be missed, with dozens of Cantonese, Szechuan and Mandarin restaurants from which to choose. Recommended, a meal of *dim sum*, meat, vegetable and fish-filled rolls and dumplings traditionally eaten for brunch.

Speaking of tradition, the Chinese New Year, between January and March, is an event to mark on the calendar. The celebration lasts a full week, and spills over to every street in Chinatown, with parades, papier mâché floats, marching bands and a block-long dragon weaving in and out of the crowd.

All year round, scents of ginger and ginseng perfume the community, while swirling incense is present both in the largest Buddhist Temple in the U.S., **Buddha's Universal Church**, and in the local Roman Catholic house of worship,

The Ceremonial Gateway to Chinatown.

Various views of Chinatown.

the **Old St. Mary's Church**, constructed in 1854 from a cargo of brick which circled Cape Horn to San Francisco. The church survived the earthquake of 1906 and a fire in 1966. An inscription on the façade reads, ''Son Observe Time and Fly from Evil''.

The Chinese Historical Society of America is the place to go for a fascinating glimpse into Chinatown's past. By 1850, there were already 4,000 Chinese, mainly from Canton, in the present area; their numbers were to increase in the following decades as they came to work in mines and on transcontinental railroad lines. The industrious Chinese soon set up their own businesses, and were initially subject to local discrimination. Not surprisingly, this brought retaliation in the form of gangs of strong-armed hatchet men, known as ''Tongs''. By the 1920s, such rivalry had come to an end, and Chinatown settled down, always absorbing new immigrants, up to the most recent influx of Vietnamese.

The crowded streets of North Beach, famous for its characteristic eateries and gourmet shops.

NORTH BEACH

The northermost limit of Chinatown is delineated by **Broadway**, a no-man's-land of porn cinemas, strip joints, and neon. However, the true boundary between Chinatown and the next ethnic neighborhood, North Beach, lies in Columbus Avenue. The latter is also the proud home of poet Lawrence Ferlinghetti's **City Lights Bookstore**, still a stronghold of the Beat Generation and the similarly-minded. Next comes **North Beach** itself, which can be best described as a mixture of Little Italy (with 100,000 residents of Italian origin), and New York's Soho (writers, poets, musicians and artists of various nationalities, some of whom specialize in San Francisco's distinctive wall murals). Many people frequent the district's jazz clubs, cabarets, and bistros in the evening.

Above, *Broadway at night, in the adult entertainement district.*
Alongside, *the Church of Sts. Peter and Paul in North Beach.*

North Beach, paradoxically, is landlocked; its name derives from the fact that it was once bordered by an inlet of the San Francisco Bay. Today, it is known for its gastronomic delights; a host of delicatessens have sprung up, wonderfully stuffed with prosciutti, provoloni, salami, mozzarella, extra-virgin olive oils and wines. The local bakeries are renowned for their **sourdough bread**. Typical of San Francisco, this is a crusty loaf made from flour and liquid fermented until sour. If that weren't tempting enough, local cafés are redolent with espresso coffee, cappuccino, and Italian pastries.
People-watching in North Beach can also be an amusing pastime, one best accomplished from a park bench in Washington Square, which is flanked by the **Church of Sts. Peter and Paul.**

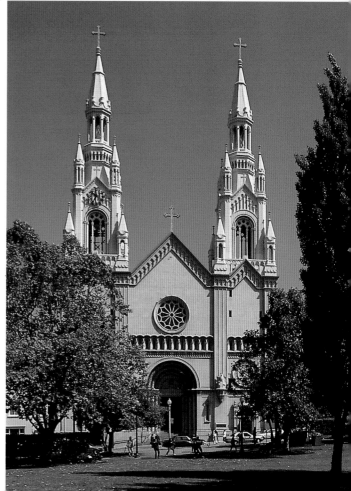

The statue of Christopher Columbus and Coit Tower.

The murals painted in 1933 by local artists on the ground floor of Coit Tower.

Panorama of Telegraph Hill.

THE HILLS

First and foremost, San Francisco is a city of hills: **Nob Hill**, former home of the "nabobs", the Gold Rush and railroad barons, now an extremely elegant residental area, and **Telegraph Hill** (284 feet), where the first telegraph station in the West was placed, in 1853. Telegraph Hill was mostly uninhabited (except by goats) until the early 1900s when Irish and Italian immigrants as well as writers and artists arrived to claim it. The upscale Bohemians have remained, in a sort of Greenwich Village on a hill dotted with frame homes and apartment buildings often perched on rocky inclines. Telegraph Hill's most outstanding landmark is **Coit Tower**, which has an interesting story behind it. The money used to build the Tower was a bequest from San Francisco eccentric Lillie Hitchcock Coit, a fan of firefighters, so much so that she became an honorary member of Knickerbocker Engine Company 5. Lillie always wore the badge the firemen gave her, and generally attended the annual firemen's banquet. The tower which was erected in 1933 at the summit of Telegraph Hill is

"The Crookedest Street in the World", Lombard Street.

210 feet high and appropriately resembles a fire-hose nozzle. Murals of contemporary California working life of the 1930s decorate the inside walls, and an elevator takes the visitor up to an observation platform and a view of the Bay. The architect of City Hall, Arthur Brown Jr., designed this San Francisco monument.

No less famous than Telegraph Hill is **Russian Hill**, which received its name from the fact that a section was used as a burial ground for Russian sailors. Writers and intellectuals have been traditionally drawn to Russian Hill, which is known for its sweeping vistas, steep paths, open green spaces, and innovative architecture.

The much-photographed "crookedest street in the world", **Lombard Street**, is found on Russian Hill; the amazing hairpin curves are carefully landscaped with bushes and flowers, making a ride down it an esthetic experience as well as a trip to satisfy one's sense of adventure.

Obviously, the hilly terrain of San Francisco caused no end of transporation problems, which the natives, ingeniously, were able to overcome, as seen in the next chapter.

CABLE CARS

On August 1, 1873, the first San Francisco cable car wound its way up Nob Hill with its inventor, Andrew Hallidie, at the grip. Four years earlier, Hallidie, a Scottish engineer, witnessed an unfortunate accident which caused a team of horses and a carriage to roll backwards on a steep cobblestone city street. This prompted him to come up with a more humanitarian (and of great importance later: pollution free!) method of getting around San Francisco. An immediate success, the San Francisco cable car system expanded to include eight lines running on 10 miles of track and 600 operating cars. The earthquake destroyed much of the network, which was never rebuilt. Yet the cable car, an essential part of San Francisco life, continued to operate, and was declared a National Historic Landmark in 1964. **Three lines** exist today, **the Powell-Hyde, the Powell Mason, the California**, with 37 cars

running on 17 miles of track, some on its place of origin, Nob Hill. The ride is a steady 9½ miles an hour, enlivened by the maneuvers of the grip man, who pulls a lever backwards allowing it, through a slot, to fasten a pincer-like hold on the continuously-running cable below street level. The cable is wound and threaded in the **Cable Car Barn**, Washington and Mason Streets, where the restored antique 1887 premises also contain historic cable car exhibits and memorabilia. Clang, clang — you hear a gripman ring the bell in his own distinctive way, and you know a cable car is coming, doubtlessly packed full of people, some hanging on from outside. The system was completely refurbished from 1982 to '84, the cars given a new maroon and gold paint job. Yet some things never change: with no reverse built into the system cable cars have to be manually turned around on turntables at the end of the line.

Half the fun in going to San Francisco is a cable car ride; at the end of the line each cable car must be manually turned around on turntables.

Left, *another view of the cable car.*
On this page, *the new building of the Museum of Modern Art, designed by Mario Botta.*

THE MUSEUM OF MODERN ART

The Museum of Modern Art of San Francisco, which opened in 1935, has a collection that includes works by the most important twentieth-century artists, such as Henri Matisse, Georges Braque, Vasily Kandinsky, Joan Miró, Jackson Pollock, Robert Rauschenberg, Paul Klee, Picasso, Andy Warhol, Georgia O'Keeffe, as well as California artists such as Richard Diebenkorn, Elmer Bischoff and David Park. All the major artistic currents of the 20th century are represented, from the Fauves and the German Expressionists to American abstract expressionism. Among the sculptors we find Giacometti, Brancusi and Arp. In 1995 the Museum moved to its new headquarters, designed by the architect Mario Botta and characterized by a cylindrical skylight 38 meters high so that the light streams down from above into the ground floor atrium.

33

Left, above, *an aerial photograph of Alcatraz with the city in the distance.*
Below, *ruins of a prison building and the interior of the penitentiary.*

"The Rock", Alcatraz.

ALCATRAZ

The freedom of the cable car ride provides a vivid contrast to an ominous-looking island in the background: **Alcatraz**. Though not in use as a federal penitentiary since 1963, the name is still enough to send chills down one's spine. The 1½ acres comprising the island is pure stone, hence the nickname "The Rock"; currents around it are strong and the water freezing cold. It was presumed no one could escape from Alcatraz; and no one ever did, alive.

Alcatraz was turned into a maximum security prison in 1934, at the height of the gangster era. Al Capone, Pretty Boy Floyd, Machine Gun Kelly and of course, the "Birdman of Alcatraz" were locked up in cells converted from military use. For Alcatraz's past has mainly been a grim one. It was the site of a U.S. Army prison during the Civil War, and the facilities were used for disciplinary purposes by the army once again during the Spanish-American War. San Franciscan prisoners were temporarily sheltered here after the earthquake.

In 1969, protesting Indians took over the island; they left in 1971. At the present time, Alcatraz is part of the Golden Gate Recreation Area, and can be reached by ferry for a guided tour. It is now a protected wildlife refuge, bringing to mind the day in 1775 when Lieutenant Juan Manuel de Ayala discovered the Rock, christening it **Isla de los Alcatraces** (Island of the Pelicans). It has always been a lonely spot. Perhaps there could be no greater punishment in the world than viewing the whole city of San Francisco, so vividly alive, from behind prison bars.

Fisherman's Wharf.

FISHERMAN'S WHARF

The feisty Dungeness crab is the logo of Fisherman's Wharf, and rightly so. Fresh seafood is what counts here: crab along with shrimp, abalone, squid, sea bass, salmon, mackerel and cod. This is what lures a small fleet of fishermen, many of whom are of Italian origin, to sail out from Fisherman's Wharf every morning at 3 am. When they return in the afternoon, there is often a crowd of onlookers to see what the catch of the day is. The colorful proceedings are augmented by the presence of vendors who serve steamed, cracked crabs out of cauldrons, along with other walkaway fish specialities. For a pleasant evening out, the area is also lined with fine seafood restaurants. Fisherman's Wharf has gotten somewhat commercial in recent years as souvenir shops, craft stands and other tourist attractions have moved in. But a certain atmosphere remains alive as you watch the fishermen tie up their boats. Something else to watch is the blessing of the fleet, which takes place in early October. The same ships herald the arrival of every New Year in San Francisco by blowing their whistles in unison precisely at midnight.

The waterfront is also home to a number of historic craft open to tours. The **Balclutha** is one such ship. She is an old three-masted square-rigger built in Scotland in 1883 which sailed around Cape Horn many times, bringing precious goods from Europe to San Francisco. As a floating museum, the Balclutha is a reminder of a glorious past. At the present, commercial shipping in the Bay area (not nearly so glamorous) has been taken over by the Port of Oakland.

Another picture of the crowded Fisherman's Wharf. Below, the Balclutha, a historical vessel, built in 1883. Right, Ghirardelli Square.

SHOPPING ATTRACTIONS

On the waterfront, smart developers successfully converted reminders of an industrial past into profitable and enjoyable marketplaces. The outstanding example is **Ghirardelli Square**. This red brick structure was the site of a woolen works until an Italian immigrant, Domenico Ghirardelli, turned it into a chocolate factory. In the 1960s it was completely renovated so that the original premises could house modern (and often whimsical) shops, restaurants, cafés, theaters, and exhibitions. The fairytale atmosphere is heightened by the presence of a clock tower, illuminated at night, which overlooks all, including a host of strolling mimes, street musicians, puppeteers, jugglers et al., who provide on the spot entertainment. And huge bars of Ghirardelli chocolate (now made elsewhere in California) are still for sale.

The same formula was used in restoring the **Cannery**, an old Del Monte peach canning establishment dating back to 1909. Now a complex containing shops and restaurants, perhaps one of its most attractive features is outdoor concerts set in a courtyard shaded by 100-year old olive trees. Back to the water's edge, yet another entertainment/shopping/eating experience can be found in **Pier 39**, built of weathered timber from demolished piers. A colorful Venetian carrousel is the highlight of a mini-amusement park; there are over 100 shops to browse in, plus, for a change of pace, plus an exciting new aquarium called Underwater World where the visitor passes through an acrylic tube surrounded by water and sealife from local waters.

Pier 39 is also surrounded by two marinas, where numerous boats are docked. The Blue and Gold Fleet are anchored here to provide short and long sightseeing cruises of San Francisco Bay.

Left, *Pier 39, lively shopping and entertainment center.* Below, *two details of the varicolored merry-go-round, one of the many attractions on the pier.*

On this page, *a fine picture of the sea lions basking in the sun on the docks of Pier 39.*

The Palace of Fine Arts now houses a science museum.

PALACE OF FINE ARTS

The Panama-Pacific International Exposition (1915) was San Francisco's way of celebrating closer ties with the East Coast, Europe and the rest of the world thanks to the opening of the Panama Canal. Forty-three states and 25 nations participated in the event, which was held on what became known as the Marina, a former cove filled in with land not far from the Presidio.

An enterprising architect, Bernard Maybeck, designed a Roman rotunda supported by Corinthian columns expressly for the Exposition. This became known as the Palace of Fine Arts. After having been extensively restored in the 1960s, it stands like a dream vision overlooking a swan-filled lagoon. The Palace of Fine Arts is the location for the Exploratorium, a science museum with over 600 hands-on exhibits especially popular with children.

The Presidio, an old military reservation that is now a park. Inside there are artillery posts dating to the Civil War and the National Military Cemetery.

THE PRESIDIO

This old military post was founded in September 1776 by the Spaniards to defend the entrance to the bay and the Mission Dolores. In 1822, when Mexico gained her independence from Spain it became a Mexican garrison; lastly the American army took it over in 1847. During the civil war, the Presidio became a field for maneuvers with lodgings for the officers and a hospital. In 1883 it was endowed with a vast territory that was to become a park: an enormous wooded area with cypresses, acacias and eucalyptus trees in the heart of the city, the ideal place for a walk, and with the National Military Cemetery, the Presidio Army Museum, the Presidio Officers Club, a curious animal cemetery, as well as military buildings and pieces of artillery dating to the 19th century on the premises. From 1946 to 1990 the Fort was the general headquarters of the Sixth Army, but a plan for transforming the entire area into a national park got under way in 1993.

The Golden Gate Bridge is the symbol of San Francisco.

GOLDEN GATE BRIDGE

For centuries explorers repeatedly missed the opening between the narrow straits leading from the Pacific Ocean to San Francisco Bay; the area had to wait even longer for a name. This was finally conferred by John C. Fremont in 1848. He recalls this christening in his *Geographical Memoir of California:* '"To this Gate I gave the name of 'Chrysophlae' or Golden Gate, for the same reason the harbor of Byzantium was called 'Chrysoceras' or Golden Horn''.

Golden Gate, name refers both to a natural, and to a man-made wonder. The **Golden Gate Bridge** connects San Francisco to Marin County.

Designed by engineer Joseph Strauss, the bridge was opened to traffic in May 1937, a prosiac use for such a poetic structure. The Golden Gate Bridge was built to withstand gales, strong currents, and its central section rises 260 feet above the water in order to allow Navy battleships to pass under it if necessary, while over 100,000 cars cross over it every day.

At 4,200 feet, the bridge is one of the world's longest. Despite the statistic, a clear image of a graceful orange-red single span is what remains impressed on one's consciousness. When the fog rolls in, as it often does, only the 746-foot towers remain visible above the mist.

Left, a few more pictures of the Golden Gate Bridge. On this page, the statue of Joseph Strauss, the engineer who designed it, and, below, a view of San Francisco seen through the steel structures of the bridge.

On the following pages, a few fascinating panoramic views of the Golden Gate Bridge.

Above, *the Conservatory of Flowers;*
left, *M.H. de Young Memorial Museum.*

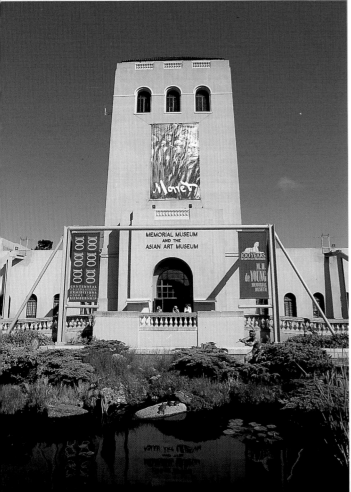

GOLDEN GATE PARK

It was a question of mind over matter. For over 50 years, from 1890 to 1943, intrepid John McLaren worked on turning 1,000 acres of sand dunes into the verdant **Golden Gate Park**. He personally planted grass, flowers, and trees (including redwoods) to create arboreta and botanical gardens out of a desolate landscape.

In the green setting that McLaren created, nearly every kind of sport imaginable can be practiced: cycling, horseback riding, boating, fishing, tennis, baseball, golf, soccer, even bowling and bocce. Man-made attractions also enrich the landscape, like the **Conservatory of Flowers**, an intricate Victorian greenhouse made in Dublin, shipped in crates around Cape Horn, and assembled in San Francisco. The Conservatory shelters tropical plants and frequent flower shows.

Publisher Michael de Young left his mark on the Golden Gate Park early in the twentieth century by spearheading a drive to establish a museum which, appropriately, is called the **M.H. de Young Memorial Museum**. Through its exhibits, the museum chronicles art in Western civilization from antiquity up to this century. A wing of the building houses the **Asian Art Museum,** which owes its existence to Avery Brundage, who donated his extensive collection of Asian art to San Francisco in 1966. As to be expected, there is a vast number of things to see, in a variety of media.

Another pull to the East can be experienced in the park's **Japanese Tea Garden**. Small bridges gracefully arch over goldfish-filled ponds here, in the vicinity of bonsai and other exotic plant species, plus, of course, cherry trees. A squat bronze Buddha, cast in China in 1790, contemplates the peaceful surroundings which are completed by the presence of a Japanese tea house.

The Japanese Tea Garden, located in Golden Gate Park.

Left, *the University of San Francisco.*
On this page, *Union Street.*

UNION STREET

In the nineteen fifties this densely-populated residential zone in Victorian style was transformed into one of the most elegant streets in San Francisco, full of refined boutiques, antique and jewelery shops, cafés and restaurants. Particularly noteworthy are the Yankee Doodle Dandy, famous for its teddy bears and traditional American quilts, Arte Forma which sells modern furniture, Enchanted Crystal and Armani Exchange. At No. 2040, the old Cow Hollow farm, after which the surroundings are named can still be seen.

HAIGHT ASHBURY

Around the end of the nineteenth century Haight Ashbury was a green area which became a tranquil residential zone in Victorian style when the area was linked to the city. It declined after the 1906 earthquake and became a densely-populated quarter, which in the 1950s began to be settled by artists and Beatniks. In 1965 the Hippies arrived en masse, attracted by the old Victorian houses and the closeness of Golden Gate Park. The Blue Unicorn Café, at the crossing between Haight and Ashbury Street, became a sort of general headquarters for their community.

*The Victorian Houses which survived
the earthquake of 1906.*

VICTORIAN HOUSES

On April 18, 1906, an earthquake measuring 8.3 on the Richter scale jolted San Franciscans out of bed before breakfast. The shock lasted only a minute, but its after-effects were devastating. Fires burned out of control for three days due to broken water mains, and entire city blocks were dynamited to check their spread. In the end, some 50,000 buildings were destroyed, and there were over 500 casualties.

San Franciscans got up and rebuilt their city with their usual indomitable spirit. A number of precious city landmarks, **Victorian Houses** remained standing, and others were rebuilt. A tribute to the carpenter's art, row upon row of these frame houses were erected in the late 1800s in four basic styles: Queen Anne, Stick, Italianate and Georgian. Elements in an individual house may include gable and turret roofs, deep recesses and bay windows, stained glass, Ionic, Corinthian and plain columns, ornately carved pediments, wooden filigree, and deep porches, all painted in strong, clear colors with white trim. But in the end, the architectural style could only be called San Franciscan.

The concrete pagoda in Japantown.

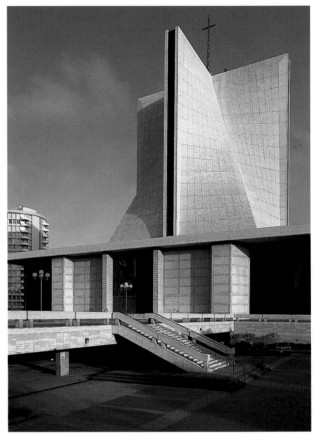

Above and on the facing page, *Saint Mary's Cathedral, designed by Piero Belluschi and Pier Luigi Nervi.*

NIHONMACHI

This is **Japantown,** a small ethnic neighborhood neatly laid out around Japanese grocery stores, restaurants, movie theatres, meeting halls and a Buddhist temple. San Francisco has strong ties to Japan; in 1957 it became a sister city to Osaka, and in 1968 a five-acre **Japan Cultural Trade Center** was formally inaugurated within Japantown. A five-tier pagoda in the Peace Plaza symbolizes friendship between eastern and western cultures; nearby is the Japanese Consulate, shops with the best of Japanese design, Japanese baths and art galleries, tempura and sushi bars. Also located near Japantown is the ultra-modern **St. Mary's Cathedral**. The striking façade is made of Italian travertine. Inside, a cascade of aluminum rods suspended above the altar is meant to symbolize the communication of prayer and the infinite flow of divine grace.

A vista of San Francisco from the city's highest point, Twin Peaks; following pages, the San Francisco-Oakland Bay Bridge.

TWIN PEAKS

The best vista of San Francisco can be had from the summit of the city's second and third highest hills — **Twin Peaks**. The 360° panorama is spectacular to say the least. And in the distance one can catch a glimpse of the **San Francisco-Oakland Bay Bridge,** a silvery span that is the world's longest steel bridge, and an impressive sight.

*Six characteristic pictures of
the streets of San Francisco.*

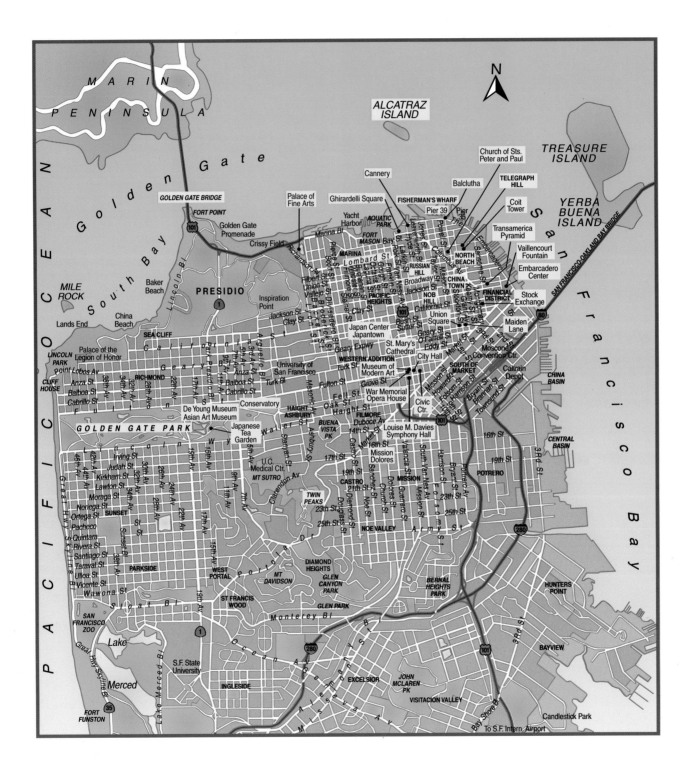

MARIN PENINSULA

ALCATRAZ ISLAND

TREASURE ISLAND

YERBA BUENA ISLAND

Golden Gate

Church of Sts. Peter and Paul

Cannery

Balclutha

TELEGRAPH HILL

GOLDEN GATE BRIDGE

Palace of Fine Arts

Ghirardelli Square

FISHERMAN'S WHARF

Coit Tower

FORT POINT

Yacht Harbor

Pier 39

Pier 35

Transamerica Pyramid

Vaillencourt Fountain

Golden Gate Promenade

AQUATIC PARK

Powell St

NORTH BEACH

Embarcadero Center

Crissy Field

Marina Bl

FORT MASON

Bay

Lombard St

RUSSIAN HILL

Broadway

CHINA TOWN

Stock Exchange

MARINA

FINANCIAL DISTRICT

MILE ROCK

South Bay

PRESIDIO

Filbert St

Union St

Vallejo St

PACIFIC HEIGHTS

Jackson St

NOB HILL

Maiden Lane

Baker Beach

Inspiration Point

California St

Union Square

China Beach

Jackson St

Clay St

Clay St

Bush St

Sutter St

Lands End

Japan Center Japantown

Geary St

O'Farrell St

Eddy St

St. Mary's Cathedral

Mosconé Convention Ctr.

SEA CLIFF

Japantown

City Hall

SOUTH OF MARKET

Caltrain Depot

LINCOLN PARK

Palace of the Legion of Honor

Geary Expwy

WESTERN ADDITION

Turk St

Museum of Modern Art

CHINA BASIN

Point Lobos Av

RICHMOND

Turk Bl

Fulton St

Grove St

War Memorial Opera House

Civic Ctr.

CLIFF HOUSE

Ariza St

Balboa St

Cabrillo St.

Conservatory

Oak St

HAIGHT ASHBURY

Haight St

FILMORE

Louise M. Davies Symphony Hall

CENTRAL BASIN

De Young Museum Asian Art Museum

Fell St

Duboce Av

GOLDEN GATE PARK

Japanese Tea Garden

BUENA VISTA PK

14th St

Mission Dolores

Irving St

Judah St

U.C. Medical Ctr.

MT SUTRO

17th St

19th St

MISSION

POTRERO

Kirkham St

Lawton St

Moraga St

TWIN PEAKS

CASTRO

21st St

Noriega St

SUNSET

23rd St

25th St

NOE VALLEY

Army St

HUNTERS POINT

Pacheco

Quintara St

Rivera St

Santiago St

Taraval St

Ulloa St

PARKSIDE

WEST PORTAL

DIAMOND HEIGHTS

Vicente St

Wawona St

MT DAVIDSON

GLEN CANYON PARK

BERNAL HEIGHTS PARK

Sloat Bl

ST FRANCIS WOOD

GLEN PARK

SAN FRANCISCO ZOO

Monterey Bl

Lake Merced

BAYVIEW

S.F. State University

INGLESIDE

EXCELSIOR

JOHN MCLAREN PK

FORT FUNSTON

VISITACION VALLEY

Candlestick Park

To S.F. Intern. Airport